"Magic?" said Kanga, walking over to look. "Ah, my dear, you're right. Fireflies lighting up the night do seem magical."

Roo hopped out from under his covers.

"Mama, can we go see them, please?"

Kanga thought for a moment.

"I suppose there's no harm," she said. "They are rather wonderful. I'd like to see them, too."

Outside, Roo jumped for joy at the fireflies as they flickered and flashed in the night.

"Wow!" he cried. "They're so beautiful."

Then, one by one, the fireflies were gone.

"Where do you think they went, Mama?" asked Roo.

"Home to bed, I hope," Kanga replied. "Just where a certain little Roo should be," said Kanga.

"But I'm not sleepy," said Roo. "And I want to know what that sound is."

"What sound?" asked Kanga.

"The singing sound," said Roo. "I think it's coming from the stream. Please, Mama, can we go find out?"

"Just this once," said Kanga. "I am curious, too."

At the stream, the singing grew louder.

"What do you think is making all those sounds?" asked Roo.

"I don't know," said Kanga. "I'm having a bit of trouble seeing in the dark. Perhaps if we stood on the bridge, whatever it is will show up."

As Kanga and Roo got comfortable on the bridge, a voice from the dark said, "Hello!"

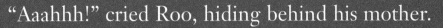

"Aaahhh!" cried Roo, hiding behind his mother.

"Don't worry, Roo. It's me," said Owl, stepping out into the moonlight. "Don't you just love the frogs' night song?"

"So that's what's making that lovely deep sound," said Kanga.

"Come, I'll show you," said Owl. Then moving as quietly as they could, Owl, Kanga, and Roo went down by the reeds that grew along the stream. There they found small frogs, big frogs, and even some toads, all croaking out their songs.

"Come, Roo," said Kanga. "It's time for us to go home."

"But what about that other sound, Mama?" asked Roo. "The chirpy one. What's that?"

"Crickets," said Owl, "are rubbing their wings. That's how they make that sound."

"I sure miss a lot when I'm sleeping," said Roo. "Who else is up right now?"

"Rabbit is," said Owl.

Roo's eyes grew big and round.

"Rabbit doesn't sleep at night?" he asked.

"I shouldn't think so," said Owl. "His eyes are made to see in the dark, just like mine. You can get a lot done when the sun goes down."

"Can we visit Rabbit?" asked Roo. "Please, Mama. Please."

"Yes," Kanga said with a smile. "I should like to see him, too."

Sure enough, when Kanga, Roo, and Owl reached Rabbit's house, they found him standing in the middle of his garden.

"Rabbit!" cried Roo. "What are you doing?"

"Trying to keep those pesky raccoons from eating my vegetables," he grumbled.

"Raccoons," said Roo, "with the masked eyes? Oh, I would like to see some of those."

"Have a seat," said Rabbit. "It's only a matter of time until they get here."

Sure enough, once everyone was quiet, a whole family of raccoons came along.

Rabbit got up to chase them off, but Roo tugged on his arm.

"Please, Rabbit, I've never seen raccoons before. I want to see what they do."

"I told you what they do," said Rabbit rather unhappily, but he stood there just the same.

As everyone watched, the raccoons headed toward Rabbit's cornstalks and began to help themselves.

"I can't look," said Rabbit, covering his eyes.

"We need to be going anyway," said Kanga. "A certain little fellow must be tired by now."

"Not really, Mama," said Roo, hiding a yawn behind his paw. "Can't we see who else is up when I'm asleep? Please?"

"There's a lovely opossum that lives over by Pooh," said Owl.

"I should like to see her," said Kanga.

"Oh, yes! Oh, yes! Oh, yes!" cried Roo.

Kanga, Roo, and Owl were on their way to Pooh's house, when Piglet
ran up, carrying his pillow and blanket.

"Piglet," said Kanga, "is something wrong?"

"Yes. I mean no. I mean...a horrible smell woke me up," said Piglet.
"And then I heard something outside my window. So I held my breath and
when it got quiet, I decided to run to Pooh's house."

"Hmmm," said Owl knowingly. "Horrible smell in the
middle of the night? I'm certain you had a visit from a skunk."

"A skunk!" cried Roo. "That sounds wonderful! I've never
seen a skunk at night."

"Then look right there," said Owl, pointing into the Wood.

"Hold your noses!" cried Piglet.

"Skunks only spray their scent when they are trying to protect themselves," said Owl. "And so far, he doesn't see us."

Piglet took off, running. "Let's keep it that way!" he cried.

"I think maybe he knows we're here," said Kanga, holding her nose, too. "Piglet had a good idea."

So Kanga, Roo, and Owl followed Piglet to Pooh's house, holding their noses and beak all the way.

When they reached Pooh's door, Piglet asked, "Are you planning on sleeping here, too?"

"No, dear," said Kanga. "We've come to look for the opossum that lives near Pooh's house."

"She's only out at night," said Roo. "So I am staying up late just to see her."

"Maybe Pooh would like to meet her, too," suggested Owl, flying off to look for the opossum.

"Hello, there," said a very sleepy Pooh as he answered his door. "Is it morning already?"

"No," said Roo, "but if you want to meet an opossum you have to come now."

Suddenly Owl appeared in the sky. "Hurry!" he called. "Opossums like to travel at night, and this one is on the move."

As Owl called out directions to his friends, Piglet, Pooh, Roo, and Kanga zig-zagged this way and that through the Wood, following the opossum.

"Where do you think she's going?" asked Roo.

"To the stream," guessed Pooh. "If she's only out at night, she must need a drink."

"Or maybe she's looking for food," said Kanga. "If she's only out at night, she must need to find food—especially for her young ones."

"I think she's headed for Pooh's Thinking Spot," said Piglet. "If she's only out at night, this must be her time for thinking."

But just as the opossum reached Pooh's Thinking Spot, she fell over and stayed perfectly still.

"What's she doing?" asked Roo.

"Playing possum," answered Owl as he landed. "Opossums do that when they want to be left alone or they're frightened."

"Let's all play possum!" whispered Kanga, giving Piglet, Pooh, and Owl a wink. As all the friends got down on the ground, Roo curled up next to his mother. Soon, Roo wasn't moving at all.

"Roo, are you sleeping?" whispered Kanga. There was no answer. "At last," she said with a smile.

Creatures of the Night

There's a world of animals that keeps busy at night. Some, like bats, move around using sound waves to guide them. Others, like rabbits, owls, and cats, have eyes designed for seeing in the dark.

Young children learn through observation, discussion, discovery, listening, and questioning. Take a nighttime safari around the neighborhood and introduce your little ones to the animals and insects of the night.

What you'll need:
- A pad
- A pencil
- A flashlight
- Brightly colored or neon-marked clothing
- Listening ears

Step 1: After the sun goes down, go for a walk around the neighborhood with an adult.

Step 2: Listen for sounds like chirping, trilling, and buzzing. Write down the sounds you hear.

Step 3: Watch for animals and insects out at night. Make a list of what you see. Different neighborhoods will have different animals.

Step 4: At home, see if you can identify the animals and their sounds. Example: an owl hooting.

Step 5: Try to get out one night a week for several weeks. See how many animals and insects you can add to your list.